Writings After The Collected Writings of Mark Rozen Pettinelli

Writings After The Collected Writings of Mark Rozen Pettinelli

Mark Rozen Pettinelli

CONTENTS

1

Writings After The Collected Writings of Mark Rozen Pettinelli

My google scholar profile (has free pdfs of my articles)

https://scholar.google.com/citations?user=RRcfeSEAAAAJ and My amazon author page (has all the books I published)

http://www.amazon.com/author/mark-pettinelli Notes on substack -

https://markpettinelli.substack.com/notes Youtube channel -

Mark Pettinelli - YouTube - https://www.youtube.com/@markpettinelli6900/shorts

Pay for youtube advertising

Try to think of the next youtube video that i want to make

Try to reread my articles and make mental notes so i can learn more stuff (i guess i'm not done analyzing them)

Try to analyze the books in my room so I can learn about more stuff

Try to help boston take over earth so they reward me and we don't all die (I mean seriously, I would be tortured for eternity by some other country) (i have no clue what some other country would do, i get along with americans). (I would certainly be tortured for eternity by some other country, I want to stick with the united states i mean seriously) THey like me, so decide to not torture me. Actually they've been torturing me i'm trying to figure this out. No what they've been trying to help me i think. I don't really understand. Anyway i want the united states to win so we all don't get killed or tortured right? This is serious stuff.

Heaven doesn't exist:

It is obvious i think, how could a heaven exist anyway a, and b, how would someone get there after they die? It might make sense to transfer a person before they die, but that wasn't what was implied by going to a heaven before anyway.

So where would this heaven be, and how could anyone get there if they are dead? Like i said already, it might make sense that they can get there before they die, if the technology was advanced enough (like how it might be today), however they have believed in heaven throughout history when there was no such technology.

Maybe i shouldn't rest my case so quickly, that is a fairly brief explanation I guess. However brief, I think it is obvious. Furthermore, why would anyone want to be permanently dead anyway? That is just stupid, if you kill yourself you are going to be permanently dead. I think it is much smarter to accept the reality on earth (no matter how hard it is) and try to stay alive, or calculate how you could stay alive for eternity anyway.

I think smart people would figure out how they could stay alive (and even help the government win the war so they can remain prosperous). THat makes sense to me, I mean why would anyone want to permanently kill themselves anyway? That is just stupid, there is a perfectly fine and real (and existing) reality on earth that we know we have for certain.

The American military also has to take over earth - this is just basic logic. Of course they have to do it in a way that doesn't end life on the planet, but nevertheless they still have to take over. I think that presents a big problem for cyber command and the army, but i hope that they can do it so we don't eventually get taken over ourselves right?

I mean, i don't know a lot about military tactics, but what were we going to do, seriously, form a diplomatic solution with all the other militaries on earth? That doesn't even make any sense, the other militaries want to hurt us, there is no other option but to take them over. ANd you know honestly, i think we will be a much kinder government to them then if they take us over. I'm just being honest and serious, how did i figure this out if I am not smart. WEll there is a global energy right, it is easy to tell that we need to take over. Our military has to fight so we can get that energy, this all makes sense to me.

I mean, maybe I am repeating myself here, but we really need to take over earth, I think it is the only security solution. Some other country would just torture me indefinitely, i thought we were friends, i mean, i know i don't know how to interact with people but seriously, we get along, i would not get along with people in other countries. And honestly, if you want to torture people, why don't you just get people in other nations not someone you supports you and has been helping you like myself, i mean like seriously. Get your act together.

I also think that the only solution is for us to become logical, this makes sense, my mind is logical but it is a simple mind. I am completely logical. I don't know why people with more complicated minds cannot be logical, but it seems like if they are trying to figure out academics so we can take over earth, our top priority is for us to become logical and intelligent so we can solve the problems we need to solve in order to take command and take over earth right.

I mean, seriously, did you want everyone in the country to die or be killed by some foreign military? If there is a foreign military, and if our large and powerful military is unable to deal with it, then what are we going to do? Raising shields around the country with a golden dome is not going to protect us forever.

If it's not, then we need to make sure the entire military can and will, and potentially go on offensive maneuvers right. That would seem to make sense. Heck, i think it just needs to flat out take over the entire planet, I don't know how long that is going to take. Unless they can make the shield be impenetrable, but I don't know how that works. Maybe military experts can figure out what the right thing to do is, I'm just offering my opinions here.

So we need to become logical then so the country doesn't end and we can take over earth, I did study logic so maybe i can offer some opinions on that then. Logic in general is truth, truth can be applied in different subject areas, but there is also truth in general right. Truth is anything accurate, or that accurately represents reality, while truth in a subject area is that type of specific knowledge that is accurate.

I mean, logic is interesting, how is someone supposed to become completely logical? Like I said, I think that the next big objective for the country is to make everyone logical. Then maybe they could figure out what they need to and solve the problems they need to solve. That makes perfectly good sense I think. Now how are we supposed to go about doing that exactly anyway?

Logic is rational thought right, and all that means is that logic is accurate or good reasoning then. How are people supposed to have all of their thoughts be accurate and reasonable then? I am completely logical for instance, all of my thoughts are reasonable and logical I know that and understand that to be correct.

What is necessary for all of someone's thoughts to be accurate and reasonable. You know, I know how it works for my mind because I have a simple mind. I can easily follow all of my thoughts and even keep track of all of my feelings, it is easy for me. I don't know how it would be for someone with a more complicated mind because I have no idea how those people's minds work anyway.

What else can I say about that then? A thought is a thought, and a feeling is a feeling, I have thoughts and I have feelings right, they are both logical I know and understand, so I would assume that just having more thoughts or more feelings would make the process more complicated, but in the same way. Like I said, thoughts and thoughts and feelings are feelings, it doesn't matter how many you have because they will still be basic thoughts and basic feelings right.

I mean, a thought is a thought and a feeling is a feeling right? What else could be said about that. Emotions can influence thoughts or thought processes. That seems obvious, however how is someone supposed to know when their thoughts are being influenced by their feelings, or when their feelings are being influenced by their thoughts? Thoughts can also influence feelings right, for instance if I think something then it could change the way I feel.

That is obvious, however people don't usually notice that kind of stuff when it is occurring anyway. I try to keep track of all of my thoughts and all of my feelings so I can be on top of things and logical all of the time. That makes perfectly good sense.

So what else could be said about logic and how to get a logical mind then. There is feeling, and there is understanding right? Both of those influence what a person thinks about, understands, reasons with and comprehends.

This is making pretty good sense, for instance Thoughts are thoughts, and feelings are feelings. Thoughts are about cognitions or other types of intellectual thinking. While there are many different types of feelings. There are mental feelings, physical feelings, emotional feelings, intellectual feelings.

I could feel happy or sad or angry or upset. What is the point of having feelings anyway? I know that they can motivate us to act and understand, however that is obvious. It is good to be aware of those processes however and understand that our feelings can influence us, the way we are, the way we understand, and how we feel the world around us.

Feelings change the way we feel the world, that is obvious, however how does that happen? This seems like it is important information. How does logic relate to feeling? The next question then would be, how does understanding relate to feeling then? If someone understands something, then it is going to make them feel a certain way right. That is also obvious.

What is emotion and cognition then - or what is the nature of feelings and thoughts and their interaction? People have feelings right, and these feelings influence our thoughts. Our understandings of the world that we have influence our feelings. Understandings could be considered to be thoughts, while feelings are just things we can feel like sensations, emotions and mental and psychological feelings then.

The line from Shakespeare - 'Cry havoc, and let slip the dogs of war' is a pretty classic line, but what does it mean anyway? It seems to be impassioned or something. I mean, it is an emotional line. He is getting excited about releasing the dogs of war I guess. He is 'crying' and that is an emotional way of acting. But why does he say - 'and let slip' 'the dogs of war', I mean, he could just say, - please release the dogs of war so they may attack our enemies. He doesn't have to be so emotional about it and cry and use the word 'havoc' right? "Let slip" i guess makes sense because dogs are usually on leashes, and they could be dogs of 'war' if there is a battle going on or if they are military dogs.

That is an emotional line anyway from Shakespeare. People are emotional all of the time. Dogs are also emotional creatures, does having dogs in the line make the statement more emotional? Or is it because there is a war going on? Those are great questions I think. I mean, people are emotional a lot, there are always feelings present right. What determines the nature of a feeling, or if a feeling is felt? How can people identify their feelings and if they having those feelings and thoughts? Is it a feeling, a thought or an understanding that the person is experiencing?

Does that make sense, there is a difference between feelings, thoughts and understandings in the mind. An understanding is something that the person understandings, and that could be a thought because a person could understand their own thoughts, and it could even be an emotion because people can also understand their own emotions and feelings.

The Collected Writings of Mark Rozen Pettinelli
A Self Help and Improvement Book: Useful Psychology Information (A Critique and Integration of Personality, Social, Interaction, Communication and Well-Being Psychology)
Mark Pettinelli

Emotions, Ideas and Logic
Mark Pettinelli

www.ingramcontent.com/pod-product-compliance
Lightning Source LLC
LaVergne TN
LVHW051923051126
851857LV00021B/2120
9798256296964